GW00420618

A note for parents and teachers

First 100 Words introduces young people learning English to some of the most important basic vocabulary they will need. A variety of useful situations and contexts unify the words, making their meaning relevant and easy to remember.

Beneath headings such as *My family, At the weekend, By the swimming-pool* and *At the airport,* the words are colourfully illustrated and clearly labelled. Features on *People* and *Opposites* extend the scope and interest of the book, making it an ideal starting point for language learning.

An alphabetical list, with page references, of all the vocabulary used is given at the end of the book to reinforce the learning process.

The *First 100 Words Workbook* in this new Ladybird series provides further practice in the use of the vocabulary which has been learned in this book, giving lively, stimulating activities, puzzles and crosswords.

Further information on local Ladybird stockists
may be obtained from the International Sales Department
Ladybird Books Ltd Beeches Road Loughborough
Leicestershire LE11 2NQ UK
Telephone: + 44 509 268021   Fax: + 44 509 219158

A catalogue record for this book is available
from the British Library

Published by Ladybird Books Ltd Loughborough Leicestershire UK
Ladybird Books Inc Auburn Maine 04210 USA

© LADYBIRD BOOKS LTD 1994

LADYBIRD and the device of a Ladybird are trademarks of Ladybird Books Ltd
All rights reserved. No part of this publication may be reproduced,
stored in a retrieval system, or transmitted in any form or by any
means, electronic, mechanical, photocopying, recording or otherwise,
without the prior consent of the copyright owner.

Printed in the United Kingdom by Ladybird Books Ltd - Loughborough

First
100 Words

words by Valerie Mendes
pictures by John Lobban

Me

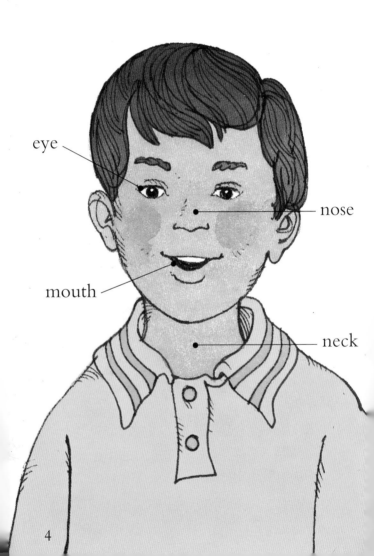

eye

nose

mouth

neck

My body

head

arm

hand

leg

foot

My family

brother
father
mother
sister
baby

My house

roof

wall

window

door

My room

desk

clock

bed

guitar

My clothes

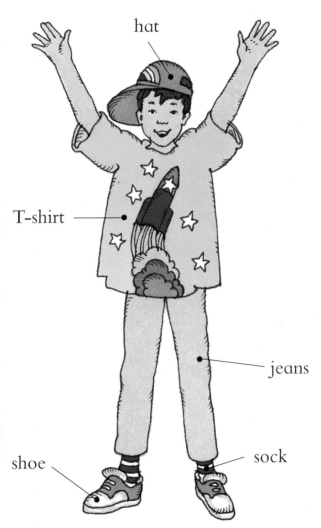

hat

T-shirt

jeans

sock

shoe

My home

bedroom

bathroom

kitchen

living-room

My food

breakfast

lunch

snack

dinner

11

tree

flower

cat

At the weekend

12

car

bus

truck

bicycle

In the street

In school

map

teacher

chalk

book

In the park

sky

tennis

ball

grass

By the swimming-pool

sun

newspaper

water

ice-cream

In the restaurant

waitress

money

air

table

At the zoo

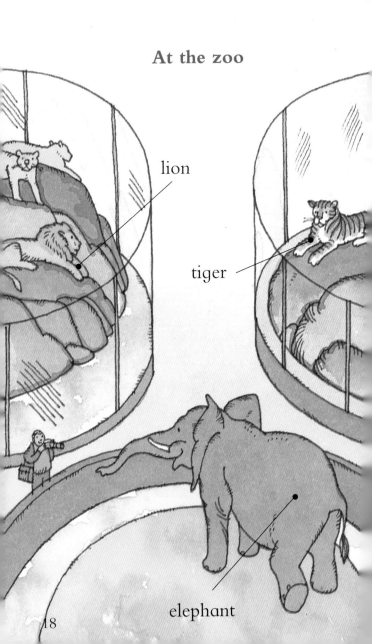

lion

tiger

elephant

Drawing a picture

paper

pencil

nt

pen

At the airport

passport

jet

tickets

suitcase

A beautiful view

sunset

mountain

road

river

A family lunch

bread

milk

cheese

butter

coffee

apple

orange

23

People

doctor

nurse

cook

actress

pilot

policewoman

driver

typist

25

Opposites

big

little

fat

thin

dirty

clean

heavy

light

happy

sad

hot

cold

Alphabetical list
of the 100 words in this book